The Joy of First Classics Book 2

For beginners and early-grade pianists.
Rare, original keyboard miniatures of three centuries.
Selected and edited by Denes Agay

Foreword

This collection is a follow-up to our singularly successful volume *The Joy of First Classics,* published only two years ago. In Book 2, the grade level is the same as in the first book (elementary to early-intermediate) but the content is entirely new and different; original, mostly rare keyboard pieces covering a period of three centuries. Many of these attractive miniatures have not been previously printed in the United States.

The pieces are in their original forms. Expression marks and fingerings were added and, in very few cases, minor editorial adjustments made to clarify the note-picture and facilitate understanding.

Denes Agay

Yorktown Music Press, Inc.

Order No. YK20568
US International Standard Book Number: 0-8256-8077-8
UK International Standard Book Number: 0-7119-1910-0

Exclusive Distributors:
Hal Leonard
7777 West Bluemound Road
Milwaukee, WI 53213
Email: info@halleonard.com

Hal Leonard Europe Limited
42 Wigmore Street
Marylebone, London, W1U 2RN
Email: info@halleonardeurope.com

Hal Leonard Australia Pty. Ltd.
4 Lentara Court
Cheltenham, Victoria, 3192 Australia
Email: info@halleonard.com.au

Printed in the EU

Contents

Dudelsack
(Bagpipe)

Old German dance
(around 1600)

Allegretto

Echo Dance

Philipp Hainhofer
(1604)

Moderato

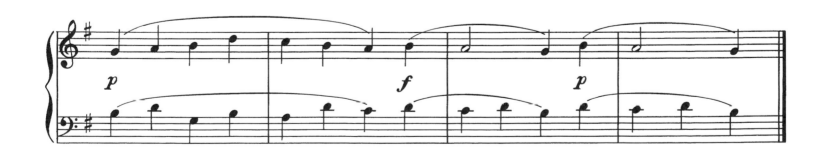

Two Little Canons

Fritz Spindler
(1817–1905)

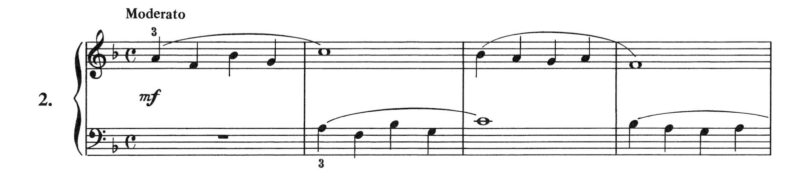

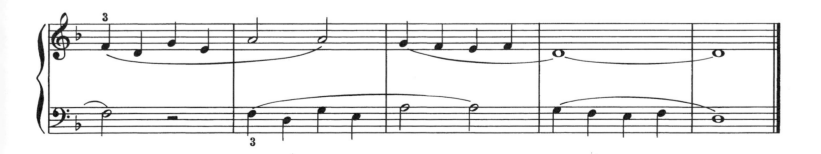

Étude Melodique

R. Ch. Martin
(France, around 1800)

D.C. ad lib.

Songful Dialogue

Thomas Attwood
(1765–1858)

Scherzino

Alexander Reinagle
(1756–1809)

Sonatina on Five Notes

Oscar Bolck
(1839–1888)

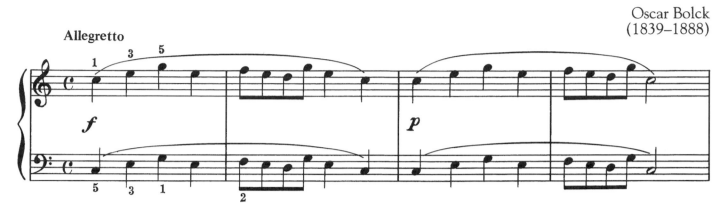

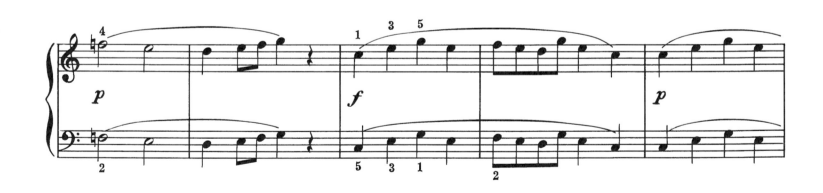

Canzonetta

Géza Horváth
(1868–1925)

Aria

Wolfgang Ebner
(1610–1665)

Duet
in Contrary Motion

Johann Friedrich Reichardt
(1752–1814)

Andante con moto

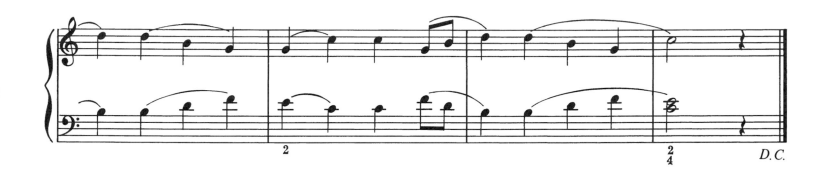

Simple Song

Alexander Reinagle
(1756–1809)

Moderato

Games

Daniel Gottlob Türk
(1756–1813)

Theme and Variation

August Eberhard Müller
(1767–1817)

Frolic

August Eberhard Müller
(1767–1817)

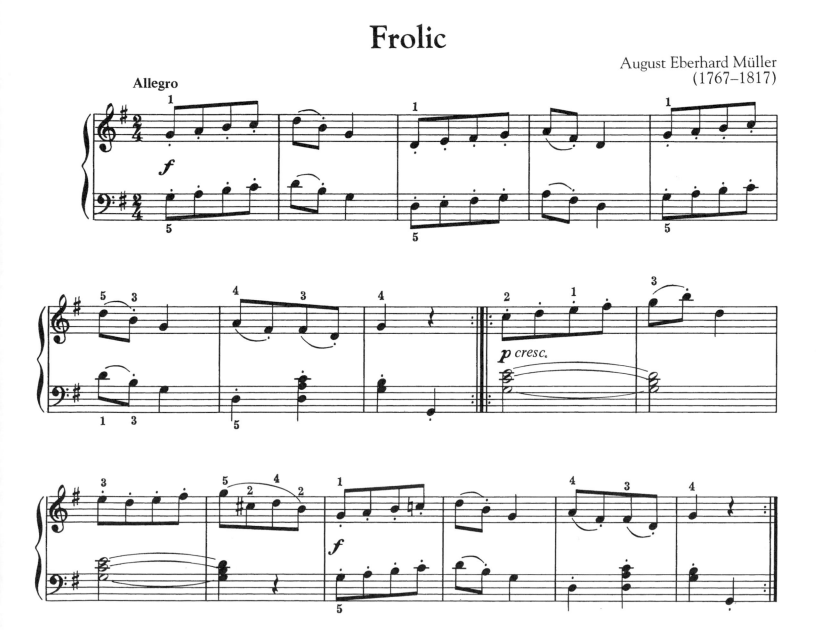

Clouds and Sunshine

Ferdinand Beyer
(1803–1863)

The Bagpipers

Alexander Goedicke
(1877–1957)

Courtly Dance

Georg Christoph Wagenseil
(1715–1777)

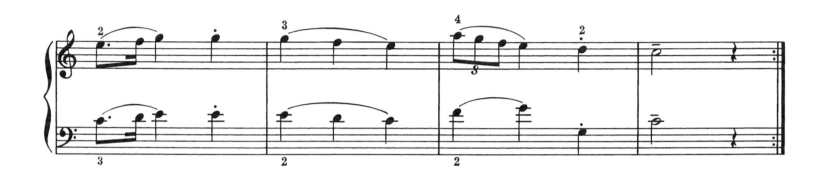

Quadrille

Joseph Haydn
(1732–1809)

At the Spinning Wheel

Louis Köhler
(1820–1886)

The Play Begins

Daniel Gottlob Türk
(1756–1813)

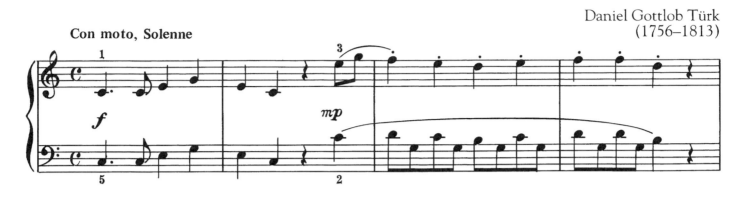

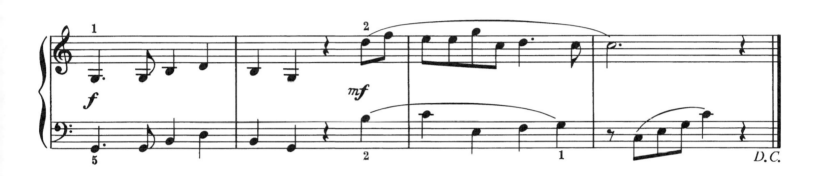

Écossaise

Friedrich Walther
(1894–?)

Hopak
Russian Dance

Alexander Goedicke
(1877–1957)

Moderately fast

Air

Wilhelm Friedemann Bach
(1710–1784)

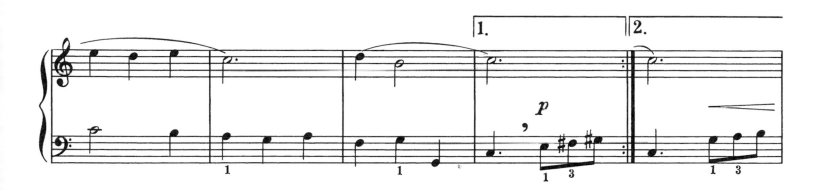

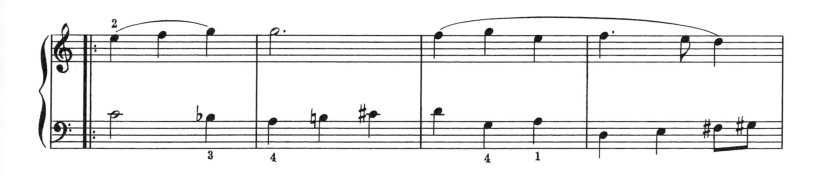

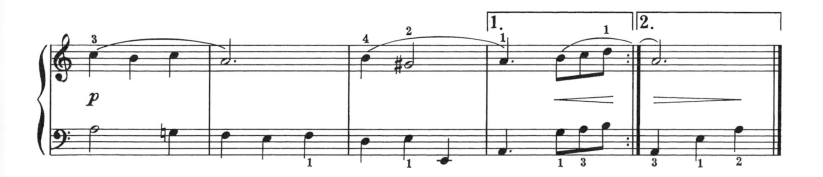

The First Minuet

Jean Baptiste Lully
(1632–1687)

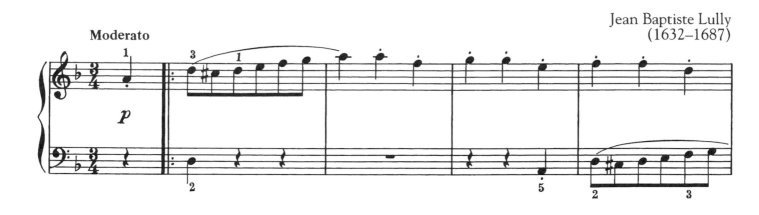

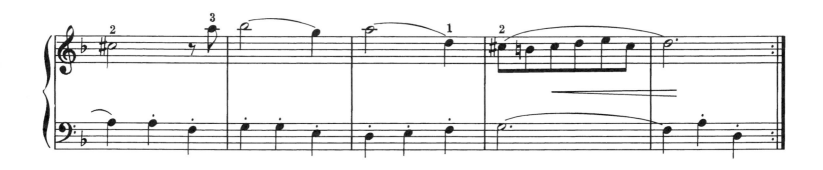

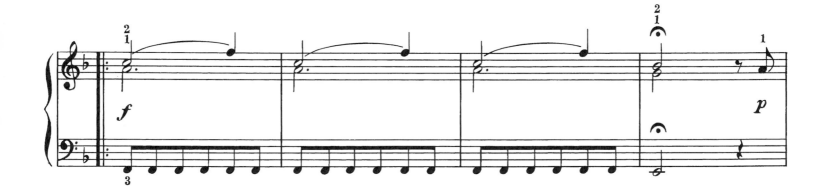

Considered to be the first published minuet in the literature.

The Village Prophet

Jean Jacques Rousseau
(1712–1778)

Tempo di Minuetto

Dialogue

Nicolas Miaskovsky
(1881–1950)

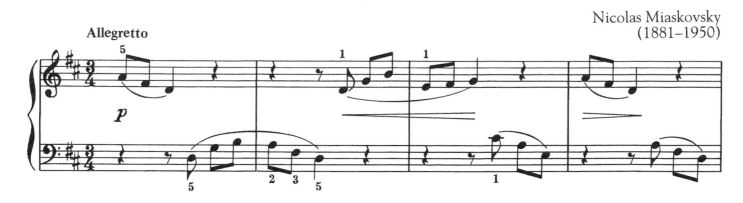

Bourdon
Hurdy-Gurdy

Michel Corrette
(1709–1795)

All ornaments are optional.

Four Little Inventions

Jan Jakub Ryba
(1765–1815)

3.

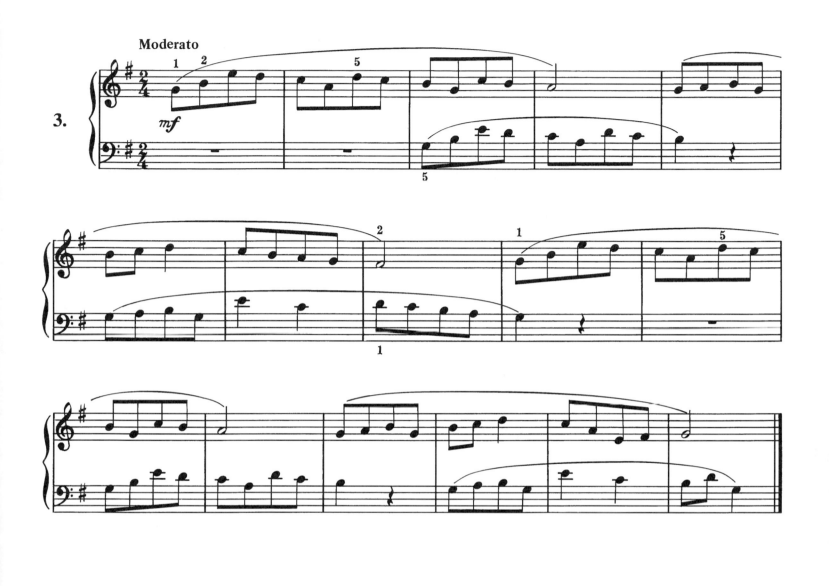

4.

Sonatina

Cornelius Gurlitt
(1820–1901)

German Dance

Joseph Haydn
(1732–1809)

Scherzetto

Alexander Reinagle
(1756–1809)

Giocoso

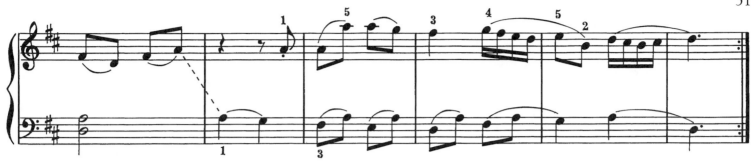

Menuette

Johann Nikolaus Tischer
(1707–1766)

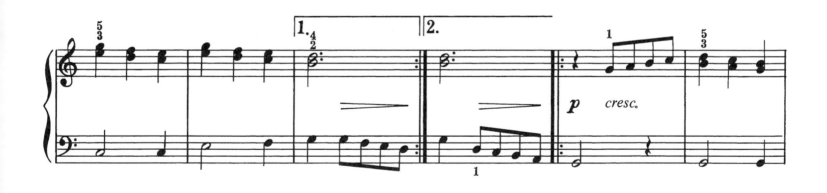

Danse Galante

Georg Philipp Telemann
(1681–1767)

Allegretto grazioso

Contredanse

Jozef Kozlowski
(1757–1831)

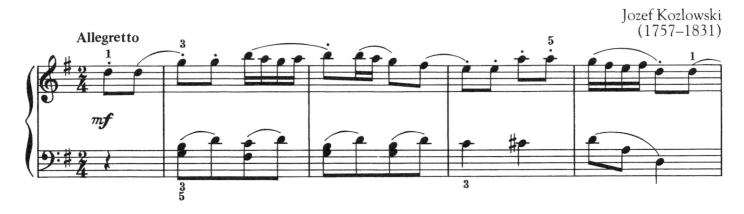

Gavotte and Gigue

Gavotte

Samuel Arnold
(1740–1802)

Andantino grazioso

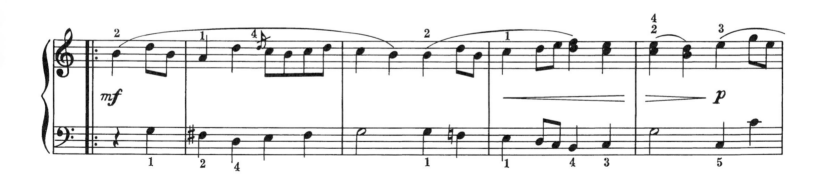

Gigue

Allegro

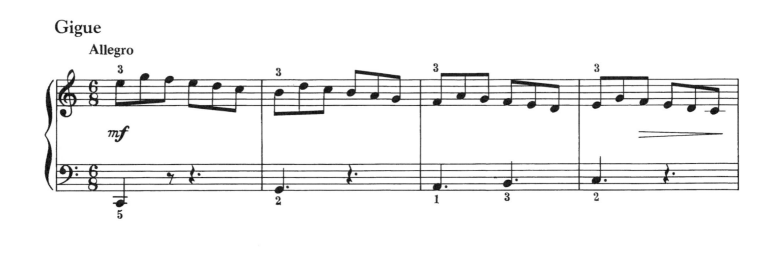

Spring Morning

William Crotch
(1775–1847)

Minuetto Scherzando

José Carlos Seixas
(1704–1742)

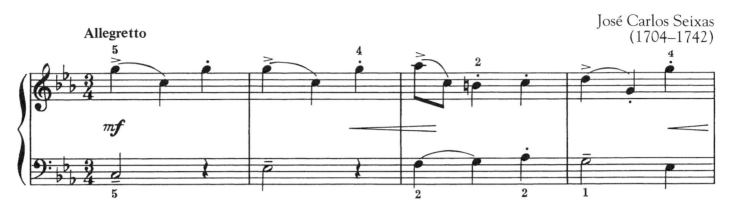

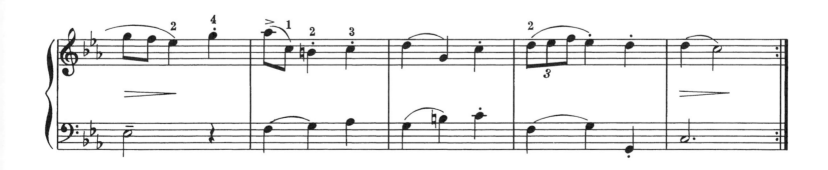

Zingarese
Gypsy Dance

Joseph Haydn
(1732–1809)

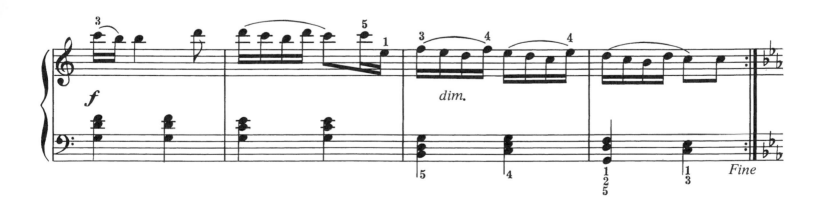

Fine

Trio

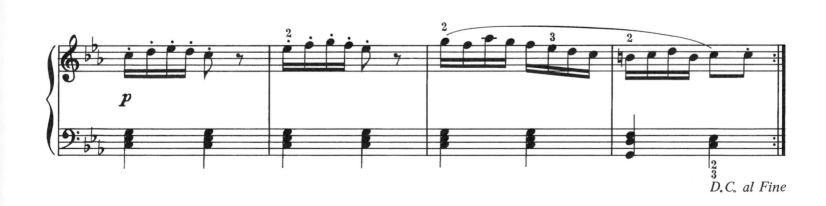

D.C. al Fine

Chaconne

George Friederic Handel
(1685–1759)

A chaconne is a variation form on a four- to eight-measure harmonic sequence. It is usually in triple meter.

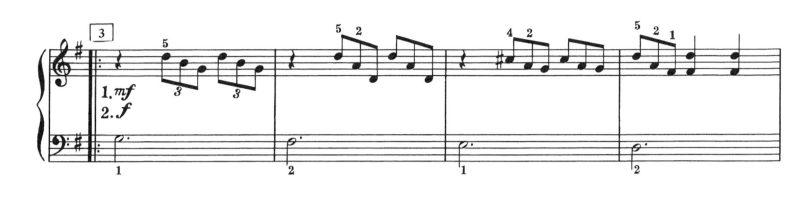

Gavotte Miniature

Ludwig van Beethoven
(1770–1827)

This piece is taken from Beethoven's sketch book.

Fandango

Louis Köhler
(1820–1886)

Ländler

Franz Schubert
(1797–1828)

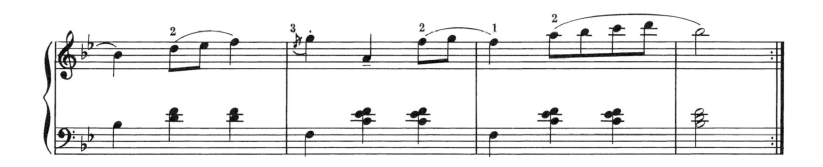

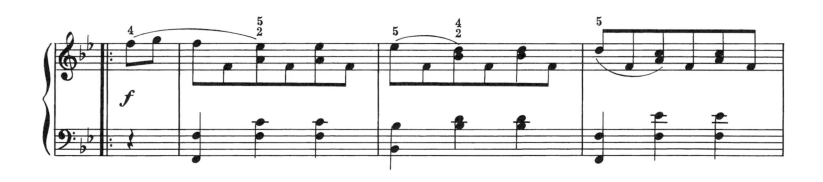

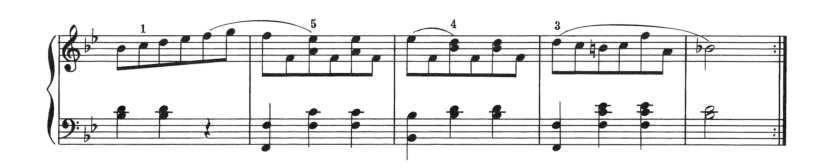

March of the Toy Soldiers

Alexander Gretchaninov
(1864–1956)

Bagatelle

Antonio Diabelli
(1781–1858)

Chanson Rustique

François Hünten
(1793–1878)

Polonaise

Sperontes (J.S. Scholze)
(1705–1750)

Andante ben ritmo

Shepherd Flutes

Bernardo Pasquini
(1637–1710)

Andantino con moto

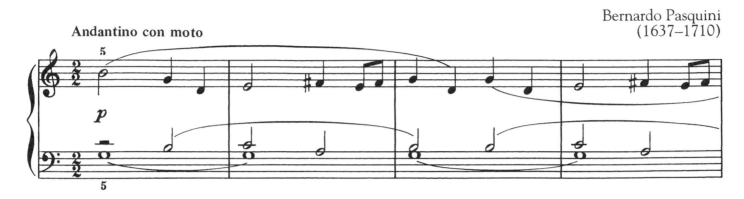

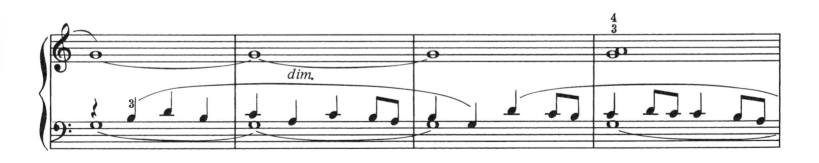

French Dance

Composer unknown
(18th Century)

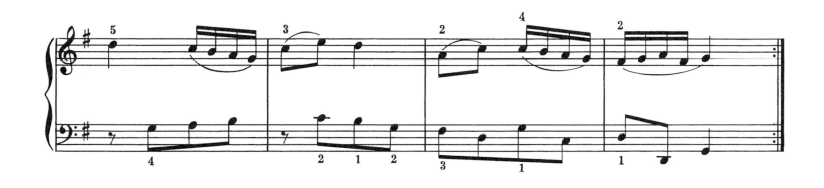

Burleska

Wolfgang Amadeus Mozart
(1756–1791)

composed in 1766.

Romanza

Daniel Steibelt
(1765–1823)

Invention

John Stanley
(1714–1786)

Gypsy Legend

Kálmán Chován
(1852–1928)

Andantino tristamente

Contredanse

Wolfgang Amadeus Mozart
(1756–1791)

Arietta

Joseph Haydn
(1732–1809)

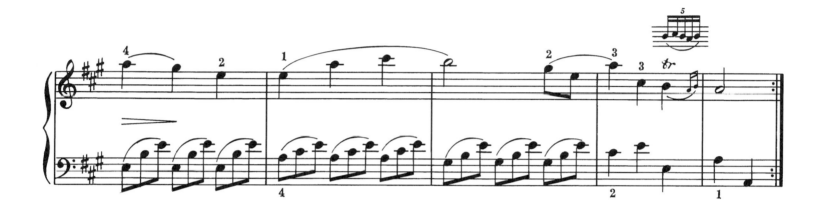

Nocturne

Johann Georg Graeff
(around 1780)

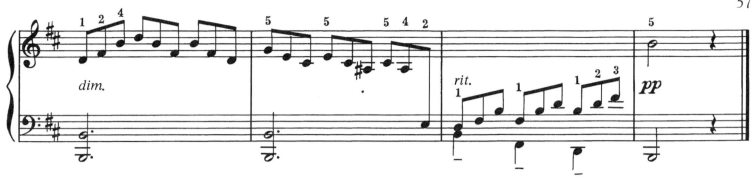

Old German Dance

Erasmus Widmann
(1572–1634)

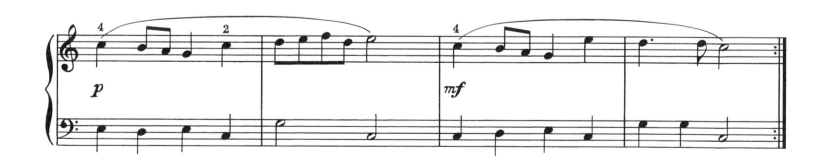

Rondo

from Sonatina Op. 157, No. 2

Fritz Spindler
(1817–1905)

Tempo I

Riding Cossacks

Antonio Diabelli
(1781–1858)

English Dance

Karl D. von Dittersdorf
(1739–1799)

First Love
from "Six Short Pieces," Op. 48

Felix Alexandre Guilmant
(1837–1911)

Preludium

Johann Anton André
(1775–1842)

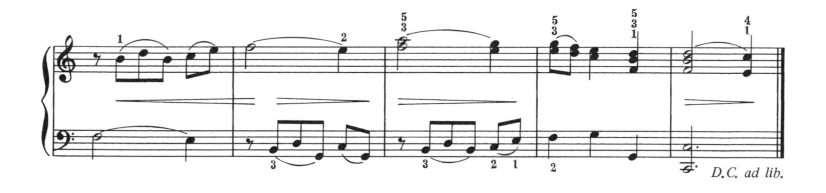

D.C. ad lib.

Gavotte and Musette

from Serenade No. 1, Op. 183

Carl Reinecke
(1824–1910)

Musette

Gavotte D.C.

Valsette

Jean Sibelius, Op. 40, No. 1
(1865–1957)

Country Waltz

Ländler

Ludwig van Beethoven
(1770–1827)

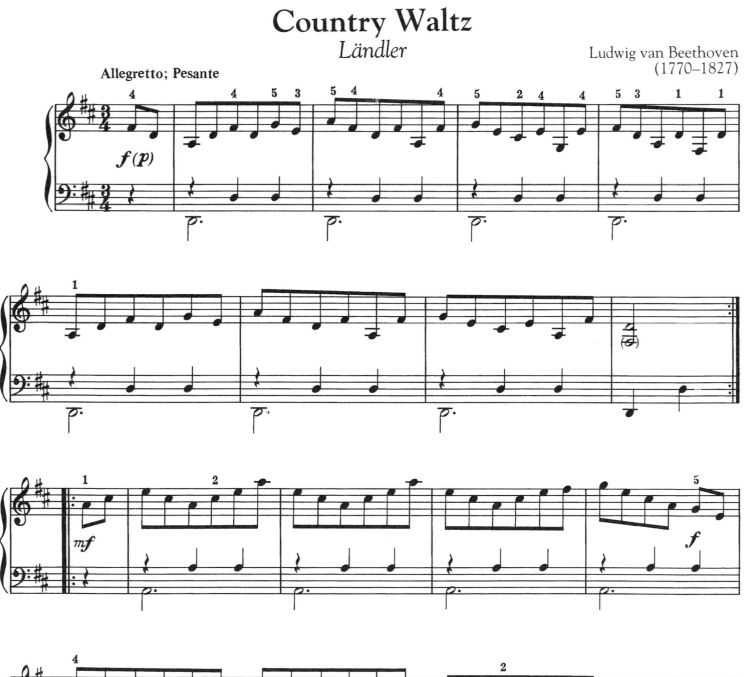

Scherzo

Carl Maria von Weber
(1786–1826)

D.C. al Fine

Sonatina

James Hook, Op. 12, No. 3
(1746–1827)

Ballet

Johann Adam Hiller
(1728–1804)

Moderato con grazia

Hungarian Soldiers' Dance

Verbunkos

János Bihari
(1764–1827)

Capriccio

Johann Adolf Hasse
(1699–1783)

Allegro

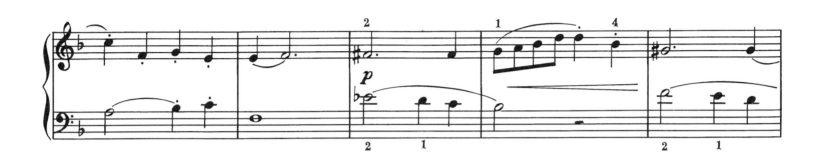

At the Playground

Carl Nielsen, Op. 53, No. 3/A
(1865–1931)

Allegro scherzoso (♩ = 112)

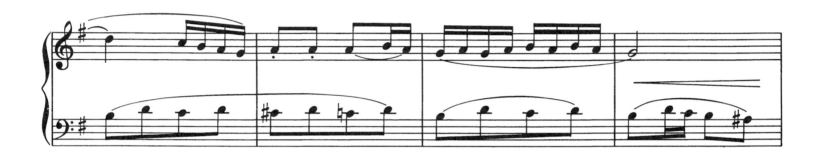

Allemande

Georg Simon Löhlein
(1725–1781)

Dedication
from Op. 1

Enrique Granados
(1867–1916)